Slut
Pop
Mimi Flood

DARK THIRTY POETRY PUBLISHING

Evolution

Aim <Shygirl♡220>

MySpace ☆Diva☆

Onlyfans.com /VenusThighTrap

Enter Your Ad Here

The blueprint. The architecture of the internet is electromagnetic.

200,000,000 different job sites to tell you, you don't have the job experience to do the bare minimum and the salary alone makes you disgusted in an instant.

Ad Want a job $40hr call 1800blahblah no experience necessary

Ad Girls Girls Girls come on and strip

3 popular social media outlets to compare your life to. Makes you happy. Lol that asshole got fat. Makes you sad. God I wish I was traveling. Doing amazing things. Makes you miss something that's not even real.

Spam Dm hey! I'm an ambassador to la-di-da. We would love for you to join us 🤍 dm to apply.

I drink coca cola and eat potato chips while looking at 30 different fat loss products to help me lose weight. I look at face creams and twenty different ads of that are on my timeline on all of my social media accounts.

Want to look 10 years younger

Be bold be beautiful with this cream

Botox free consultation

Lose 30lbs in 3 weeks

Have you ever notice everything about sex is for men. Pornhub. I would watch porn and take notes. Gag. Tell them to choke me. I don't like getting smacked in the face with a hand or dick and pretending I'm okay with it. But it's what you're taught.

All the ads

Cam girls for you

Rebecca can't wait to see you

Pay now 🤑

Milfs for you

Try not to cum 💦

Click here 👅

Everything makes you feel desensitized. Everything here makes you feel alone.

2005

Dreams about you 2005 / your clothes on my bedroom floor / a ring pop on my ring finger / I got

Sasha Grey's gagging sounds pat down/ as LimeWire downloads a virus to my computer /

Myspace its complicated status / I loved you / and some days I miss you / you look happy.

Lana Del Rey Music Video

We're in a Lana Del Rey music video/we went skinny dipping in the lake / the ribbon in my hair drifted away/ under the waning crescent/ violet clouds fall low like mountains in the night sky/ your gaze hangs in my soul / wrapped in a pink starburst of our secret

Slut Pop

Slut pop bubble pop electric / I'd rather give you bite marks down on your neck like little moons than to give you an emotional ballad / I'm not a burrow of keepsakes /but sometimes I hear men say my name during sex / and the slit of air in tires / the heartbeat of a tree /and the tiny bell of my heart.

The Spice Girls Of Emotions

Baby = Denial

Constantly lie about my own feelings to save something that is drowning/ to stare at an hourglass of sand in every room knowing how it's going to end/ while kissing / while making breakfast/ while having sex / while holding hands / asking yourself why can't I call/ text/ dm / why can't I be loved without feeling like there will be consequences

Ginger = Bargaining grief

Kate bush- running up that hill on repeat/ I wanted to eat her cancer / I remember the night sky was in Pisces/ I didn't hold her hand long enough/ I waited too much / to say goodbye.

Posh = Depression

Watch Netflix for hours/ Santa Clarita Diet / sense8/eat ice cream / cry into tissues / I think there's is something fundamentally broken within me / I think people who form relationships with me are more born from convenience than something that is genuine/ watch I'm not okay with this / never have I ever / glow / stranger things / you / eating less / sleeping less / anxiety about how I don't fit into my life / whatever I do feels wrong / love notes (period) on the bed sheet/ schitts creek/

Ginny and Georgia/ one day at a time/ the
lights flicker like a camp fire / i opened my
hand to try to catch it / dear white people/
squid game / outerbanks / the get down / the
ring around the shower drain is getting
bigger / I tried to scrub it off / I wore out the
paper towels / it disintegrated into pieces but I
kept scrubbing till my nails broke off / till my
fingertips started to bleed / watched
heartstopper / sex education/ I just wanna feel
something else / the umbrella academy /
chewing gum / dissociation/ through tv shows

Sporty = anger

(Screaming)
fuuuuuuuuuuuuuuuuuuuuuuuuuuuuuucccccccccccccc
ccccccccccccccccccccccccccccccckkkkkkkkkkkkkkkk
kkkkkkkkkkkkkkkkkkkkkkkkkkkkkkk!!!!!!! Fuck.
(On my knees) (Wipe my face with my hands)
(Even if there's dirt) (Even if it's bloody) (Even
if my reflection staring from my palms) (Now
get the fuck up)

Scary = acceptance

Sigh a breath /now you can write this.

LA Woman

I had dreams / I was going to be a big bright
star/ be a LA woman/ sit on the O of the
Hollywood

sign and take a shot when I first see my name
in the sky/ but I guess not all of us get out of
our

own way / we swim in circles / and float to the
surface like dead goldfish you win at a county

fair with a life span of a week.

Audio

(Kissing sounds).............?????...................

(Sighs   )

....
....

????????....to the

left....oooooooOOOOOOOOOOOOOOOOOOOOOOOOOOO
OOOOOOOOOOOOOOOOOOO

(Deep breathing) (Condom wrapper being ripped and put on).. (Mac and cheese sound)

Fuck.(grunts) (Moans) Cum inside me. (Encouragingly)

Pink Jelly Center

Pink jelly center and a cherry on top /when he fingers me / his eyes close when he fucks me/ I'm still here/ in a room that swallows me/ even with a crowd of people / there's a scream of loneliness/ I set a house fire inside my body /and I'm smiling and laughing/ I'm the only one who sees the exit at the bottom of the swimming pool without coming up for air/ I'm still a body of his / I'm still a body being licked by the void

Flies

My heart is sticky and prone to flies, cigarette butts, and pinky rings/ fruit flies swarm the

bathroom trash filled with tampons / even they can't wait their turn to take/ I get undressed with

a camcorder on I bought from eBay to view how much my body lost/ lay on a mattress and

finger myself till everything feels good again/ and then take forty pictures of me smiling/ pick one

and edit it put a filter over it / post it on Instagram/and insert a mediocre inspirational quote/

watch it get likes and comments.

Bimboification

Hot pink / tongues on tongues / so sweet / big
boobs / chained nails / perfection/ you will
objectify / sexualize / make a mockery / and
embarrass on what you see in night vision on
your computer screen / 2003 that's so hot /
bellybutton rings and no matter how you
spread your legs / it's a bimbo / girl you're
dumb / no bitch I'm a masterpiece

I'm Not A Virgin/ I'm An Aries

/ My blouse / my black hair / my eyes/ my body / my size / my bellybutton/my breast/ my tattoo /my mouth / my kiss / my throat / my tongue/my taste / my vagina / things one wants to see / to touch/

My intelligence/ my ambition/ my depression/ my anxiety/ my smile / my laughter / my vulnerability/ my intimacy/ my passion/ my stubbornness/things nobody wants to ask /

My tampon / my stillborn / my health / my abortion/ my blood / things nobody wants to talk about/

But the important thing: he asks if I'm a virgin/ says I walk like one/ doesn't even ask about my name.

Then asks what my body count is

Jawbreaker

15

Shape-shifting in baby doll dresses and
chatrooms/ swishes mouthwash into the sink
after oral sex and looks in the mirror / mascara
goop in a corner/ dick lips and a jawbreaker in
my pocket

Swallow

I think of you separating water from salt and pouring that salt in my bellybutton /I think of you tongue tying me breathless/ as if I saw the lost Atlantis inside you / I think of you in bits and pieces of love/ a soul with teeth and fingernails and burned down buildings and cheap liquor/ I always feel you like the air In between two stars/ I orgasm eggshell pearls / and put one in your mouth / and ask you to swallow.

Baked Dreamz

Holding a vibrator to my clit and then insert it inside for serotonin and not feeling a thing is when the static in my brain gets put to good use that I would thank an invisible God for / I take three weed gummies because I'm allergic to smoke / ran a bath and soaked /visioned :

Me dancing like Tawny Kitaen on the boy's next door 1970 Pontiac firebird.

Have a conversation with an old childhood friend drinking coffee but we're eight. In a rave floral shirt with blue pants and black shoes and she's wearing a green stripe turtle neck shirt and a lime skirt with a light purple short sleeve jacket and white sneakers. Just like in picture that I have in photo album.

Get finger fucked with pantyhose on by a guy I've seen at a bar multiple times with the ice blue eyes.

Be a lead in all the movies and tv all I love where my face and body just morph over on the screen.

Dry Britney Spears crying eyes when she dances.

Matthew Schultz marries and buries me in lyrics.

Splash a round in a martini glass and pour a
thousand dollar champagne bottle down my
body.

Win a Miss American Vampire pageant

And all the depression void monsters I drew
living in a teletubbie landscape

I want to drive on an open road with a rose
that's genetically modified behind my ear that I
buy from a gas station and I'm going nowhere
and somewhere at the same time.

Climb at the top of a Ferris wheel before it
opens on the Santa Monica Blvd and I just
stare at the sky and write.

Mimi Flood has been published in Dark
Thirty Poetry Publishing, Querencia press,
The Graveyard zine, Scar Tissue Magazine,
Gypsophila and more.

Instagram: @Marigold_Jesus